98616534R00049

Made in the USA
Lexington, KY
08 September 2018